A Prayer a Day

from Lent to Easter

David Adam

kevin mayhew

kevin mayhew

Published in Great Britain in 2008 by Kevin Mayhew Ltd
Buxhall, Stowmarket, Suffolk IP14 3BW
Tel: +44 (0) 1449 737978 Fax: +44 (0) 1449 737834
E-mail: info@kevinmayhewltd.com

www.kevinmayhew.com

9 8 7 6 5 4 3 2 1 0

ISBN 978 1 84867 076 1
Catalogue No. 1501134

Cover design by Rob Mortonson
Edited by Katherine Laidler
Typeset by Richard Weaver

Printed and bound in Great Britain

Contents

Introduction 5
The meaning of Lent 7

Ash Wednesday 11
First week of Lent – Dedication 13
Second week of Lent – Love 17
Third week of Lent – Guidance 21
Fourth week of Lent – The help of God 25
Fifth week of Lent – The power of God 28
Palm Sunday 31
Holy Week 32
Easter Day 36
Easter Week 38

Introduction

Prayer is an expression of our relationship with God. If we ignore our prayers that relationship breaks down from our side though God remains faithful to us. If we turn again to God we will discover he was waiting to come to us. The beginning may not be easy for we may have wandered far away but in our very desire to pray it is God calling us.

To pray is to become a friend of God. In prayer earth and heaven embrace each other and become one. We open our lives to God who loves us with an everlasting love. Let us not deprive ourselves of this great love. Learn to enjoy the Presence of God and so enjoy his love and his peace.

Praying is not specifically an intelligent or even a spiritual exercise but rather an expression of love for God and a desire to be aware of God's love for us. Praying is above all an act of love.

For this reason the prayers in this book were not written out of a desire to give a daily exercise but as a means to simply open oneself to the wonderful presence and love of God. They were written in love and adoration for the ever-present and ever-loving God. It is my hope that you will use these prayers to help you to become aware of God's love and to respond to it.

The best way to use these prayers is to fix a time and a place to use them. Make a meeting place each day where you can give your attention and love to God. Do not use lots of words. Choose a single prayer and stay with those words. The importance is to enjoy speaking to God and being with God. Your relationship with God is more important than any words; just use these words as an aid and learn to abide in his presence and love. Though there are many prayers in this book, they came into being over many years and through many situations. Use the ones that are most meaningful and relevant to you and above all let them lead you to speaking directly to God in your own words.

God bless you in this great venture; through him may you know the joy of the fullness of life.

David Adam

The meaning of Lent

The word Lent comes from an old English word meaning lengthening. Lent occurs at the time of the year when daylight increases and the days get longer. It is a time when we can extend our activities with the growing light. By tradition Lent is a time for extending ourselves and it is a mistake to look upon it as a time for limiting ourselves, unless that limiting frees us to do something else. To say we give up sweets or wine is trivialising Lent unless this spurs us on to do better things, such as giving to those in need or improving our relationships with God and each other.

Lent is the six weeks before Easter and its purpose is to be a time of preparing: a time when we seek to understand the fullness of Christ's offering on the cross and rejoice in the resurrection. Lent begins on Ash Wednesday and continues to Easter Eve. The last week of Lent is known as Holy Week and looks at the final acts of Jesus up to his death and burial. In the Western tradition of the six weeks of Lent, Sundays are not counted as days of Lent as they act like all Sundays, as a reminder of the day when Christ arose from the dead.

In the early Church, Lent was a time when converts were prepared for baptism. It was a time of forty days of instruction and discipline prior to baptism at Easter. At this time penitents were also prepared to be welcomed back into the Church. By the fourth century it was beginning to be realised that Lent would be a good time for all Christians to develop their faith and increase their allegiance to Christ.

The forty days of Lent are a reminder of the forty days that Moses spent on the mountain (Exodus 24:18; 34:28). It is also a reminder of the forty years the people of Israel spent in the wilderness. Elijah spent forty days on his journey to Mount Horeb after being fortified by an angel in the wilderness (1 Kings 19:8). But, above all, Lent is a reminder of the forty days Jesus spent in the wilderness and how he was tempted by the devil (Matthew 4:1, 2; Mark 1:12, 13; Luke 4:1, 2).

Lent has three main themes for Christians to consider: prayer, fasting and almsgiving. These in turn are designed to make us look at three areas of our life. Prayer makes us look again at our relationship with God. Is our relationship a vital, living part of our daily life? Lent is a time to improve our prayer life and to make sure we spend some time each day with our God. Remember that faith is not about making credal statements; it is about our relationship with God. The prayers in this book are to help us develop our relationship with God and to make contact with him each day. These prayers are to be a spur to help us enter into stillness with the God of love and, when we speak, to use our own words as well as what is written.

Fasting should make us look at how we are using the world around us and how we use time. Are we wasting God's good world? Fasting can make us look at issues like global warming and how 'slave' labour is used to produce many of our so-called cheap goods. It should make us aware of the hungry and the poor of our world. Fasting is not just giving up, for if you leave a field empty, it will fill with weeds. Fasting is about giving up so that we can give out or take on something. Fasting leads us to championing good causes and helping where aid is called for. In our consumer society, fasting can be a witness to the fact that we do not need to consume so much. Sometimes consuming is a sign of emptiness within our hearts and souls and is nothing to do with our stomachs.

Almsgiving should be a natural part of all who have received of the good of the world. Almsgiving is a sign of our generosity: as God has given us, we seek to share our good gifts with others. Sometimes people's hearts are as closed as their wallets. Almsgiving often results from prayer and fasting. The closer we come to God, the closer we are drawn to each other. This is also true the other way around for if we are insensitive to others, we can hardly be sensitive to the great Other who is God. Prayer is not something we perform in a vacuum; it involves all our relationships with God and his whole creation. Fasting, or freeing ourselves from something, gives us more time or money to dedicate to some cause and to our God.

This book is to encourage you to extend yourself, to reach out and reach for God. The wonderful thing is that God waits for us to turn to him. Remember to draw near to God and he will draw near to you.

Ash Wednesday

Almighty and everlasting God,
you hate nothing that you have made
and forgive the sins of all those who are penitent:
create and make in us new and contrite hearts
that we, worthily lamenting our sins
and acknowledging our wretchedness,
may receive from you, the God of all mercy,
perfect remission and forgiveness;
through Jesus Christ our Lord.

Collect for Ash Wednesday, Common Worship

Thursday after Ash Wednesday

Lord Jesus,
tempted to turn stones into bread,
forgive my seeking only earthly gain
and give me the vision to see
that I do not live by bread alone.
Make me aware that
I hunger for your presence
and long for your love.

David Adam

Friday after Ash Wednesday

Lord Jesus,
tempted to jump from the Temple
and tempted by words of Scripture,
teach me to put my trust only in you
for you alone are the living Word
and only you can save.

David Adam

Saturday after Ash Wednesday

Lord Jesus,
tempted to compromise by being offered great gain,
teach me that there is no gain
if I sacrifice or starve my soul
and that I should give my life to you;
who live and reign
with the Father and the Holy Spirit,
one God now and for ever.

David Adam

First week of Lent – Dedication

Sunday

Almighty God,
whose Son fasted forty days in the wilderness,
and was tempted as we are, yet without sin:
give us grace to discipline ourselves
in obedience to your Spirit;
and as you know our weakness,
so may we know your power to save;
through Jesus Christ your Son our Lord,
who is alive and reigns with you,
in the unity of the Holy Spirit,
one God, now and for ever.

Collect for the First Sunday of Lent,
Common Worship

Monday

Grant, O Lord,
that your love may so fill our lives
that we may count nothing too small
to do for you,
nothing too much to give,
and nothing too hard to bear.

St Ignatius of Loyola (1491–1556)

Tuesday

O Lord, to turn away from you is to fall,
to turn to you is to rise,
and to stand in your presence is to live for ever.
Grant us in all our duties your help,
in all our perplexities your guidance,
in all our dangers your protection,
and in all our sorrows your peace,
through Jesus Christ our Lord.

St Augustine of Hippo (354–430)

Wednesday

Lord Jesus,
I give thee my hands to do thy work.
I give thee my feet to go thy way.
I give thee my eyes to see as thou seest.
I give thee my tongue to speak thy words.
I give thee my mind that thou mayest think in me.
I give thee my spirit that thou mayest pray in me.
Above all, I give thee my heart
that thou mayest love in me
thy Father and all mankind.

Lancelot Andrewes (1555–1626)

Thursday

Lord Jesus, our Saviour, let us now come to you.
Our hearts are cold;
Lord, warm them with your selfless love.
Our hearts are sinful;
cleanse them with your precious blood.
Our hearts are weak;
strengthen them with your joyous Spirit.
Our hearts are empty:
fill them with your divine presence.
Lord Jesus, our hearts are yours;
possess them always and only for yourself.

St Augustine of Hippo (354–430)

Friday

Lord, I am no longer my own, but yours.
Put me to what you will, rank me with whom you will.
Put me to doing, put me to enduring;
let me be employed for you or laid aside for you,
exalted for you
or brought low for you;
let me be full, let me be empty;
let me have things, let me have nothing.
I freely and wholeheartedly yield all things
to your pleasure and your disposal.
And now, glorious and blessed God,
Father, Son and Holy Spirit,
you are mine and I am yours.
So be it.

John Wesley (1703–1791)

Saturday

Father, I abandon myself to you.
Do with me as you will.
Whatever you may do with me I thank you.
I am prepared for anything.
I accept everything,
provided your will is fulfilled in me
and in all creatures.
I ask you for nothing more, my God.
I place my soul in your hands.
I give it to you, my God,
with all the love of my heart,
because I love you.
And for me it is a necessity of love,
this gift of myself,
this placing of myself
in your hands without reserve
in boundless confidence,
because you are my Father.

Charles de Foucauld (1858–1916)

Second week of Lent – Love

Sunday

Almighty God,
you show to those that are in error the light of your truth,
that they may return to the way of righteousness:
grant to all who are admitted
into the fellowship of Christ's religion,
that they may reject those things
that are contrary to their profession,
and follow all things that are agreeable to the same;
through Jesus Christ your Son our Lord,
who is alive and reigns with you,
in the unity of the Holy Spirit,
one God, now and for ever.

Collect for the Second Sunday of Lent,
Common Worship

Monday

Set our hearts on fire with love for you,
O Christ our God,
that in that flame we may love you
with all our heart,
with all our mind,
with all our soul,
and with all our strength,
and our neighbours as ourselves;
so that keeping your commandments,
we may glorify you, the giver of all good gifts.

Eastern Orthodox

Tuesday

My Lord and my God, take from me
all that keeps me from you.
My Lord and my God,
grant me all that leads me to you.
My Lord and my God,
take me from myself and give me completely to you.

St Nicholas of Flue (1417–1487)

Wednesday

Look upon us, O Lord,
and let the darkness of our souls vanish
before the beams of your brightness.
Fill us with holy love,
and open to us the treasures of your wisdom.
All our desire is known to you,
and therefore perfect what you have begun,
and what your Spirit has awakened us to ask in prayer.
We seek your face; turn your face to us
and show us your glory.
Then shall our longing be satisfied,
and our peace shall be perfect.

St Augustine of Hippo (354–430)

Thursday

O Love, O God, who created me,
in your love recreate me.
O Love, who redeemed me,
fill up in me whatever part of your love
has fallen into neglect in me.
O Love, O God, who first loved me,
grant that with my whole heart,
and with my whole soul,
and with my whole strength,
I may love you.

St Gertrude (1256–c.1302)

Friday

Lord, you have taught us
that all our doings without love are nothing worth:
send your Holy Spirit
and pour into our hearts that most excellent gift of love,
the true bond of peace and all virtues,
without which whoever lives is counted dead
before you.
Grant this for your only Son Jesus Christ's sake,
who is alive and reigns with you,
in the unity of the Holy Spirit,
one God, now and for ever.

Collect for the Second Sunday after Trinity,
Common Worship

Saturday

Merciful God,
you have prepared for those who love you
such good things that pass our understanding:
pour into our hearts such love towards you
that we, loving you in all things and above all things,
may obtain your promises which exceed all that we can desire:
through Jesus Christ our Lord.

Francis Paget (1851–1911)

Third week of Lent – Guidance

Sunday

Almighty God,
whose most dear Son went not up to joy
but first he suffered pain,
and entered not into glory before he was crucified:
mercifully grant that we,
walking in the way of the cross,
may find it none other than the way of life and peace;
through Jesus Christ your Son our Lord,
who is alive and reigns with you,
in the unity of the Holy Spirit,
one God, now and for ever.

Collect for the Third Sunday of Lent,
Common Worship

Monday

O gracious and holy Father,
give us wisdom to perceive you,
intelligence to understand you,
diligence to seek you,
patience to wait for you,
eyes to behold you,
a heart to meditate upon you,
and a life to proclaim you;
through the power of the Spirit
of Jesus Christ our Lord.

St Benedict (480–550)

Tuesday

O God, the protector of all who trust in thee,
without whom nothing is strong, nothing is holy:
increase and multiply upon us thy mercy;
that thou being our ruler and guide
we may pass through things temporal,
that we finally lose not the things eternal.
Grant this, O heavenly Father,
for Jesus Christ's sake our Lord.

The Book of Common Prayer (1662)

Wednesday

Almighty and eternal God,
so draw our hearts to thee,
so guide our minds,
so fill our imagination,
so control our wills,
that we may be wholly thine,
utterly dedicated unto thee;
and then use us, we pray thee, as thou wilt,
but always to thy glory and the welfare of thy people;
through our Lord and Saviour Jesus Christ.

Archbishop William Temple (1881–1944)

Thursday

Eternal God and Father,
you create us by your power
and redeem us by your love;
guide and strengthen us by your Spirit,
that we may give ourselves in love and service
to one another and to you;
through Jesus Christ our Lord.

The Alternative Service Book (1980)

Friday

Enable us, O Lord God,
to walk in thy way with integrity and cheerfulness,
faithfully believing thy Word,
and faithfully doing thy commandments,
faithfully worshipping thee
and faithfully serving our neighbour,
in the name of thy Son our Saviour Jesus Christ.

Jeremy Taylor (1613–1667)

Saturday

O God, the protector of all who trust in you,
without whom nothing is strong, nothing is holy:
increase and multiply upon us your mercy;
that with you as our ruler and guide
we may so pass through things temporal
that we lose not our hold on things eternal;
grant this, heavenly Father,
for our Lord Jesus Christ's sake,
who is alive and reigns with you,
in the unity of the Holy Spirit,
one God, now and for ever.

Collect for the Fourth Sunday after Trinity,
Common Worship

Fourth week of Lent – The help of God

Sunday

Merciful God,
absolve your people from their offences,
that through your bountiful goodness
we may all be delivered from the chains of those sins
which by our frailty we have committed;
grant this, heavenly Father,
for Jesus Christ's sake, our blessed Lord and Saviour,
who is alive and reigns with you,
in the unity of the Holy Spirit,
one God, now and for ever.

Collect for the Fourth Sunday of Lent,
Common Worship

Monday

O God, forasmuch as without you
we are not able to please you;
mercifully grant that your Holy Spirit
may in all things direct and rule our hearts;
through Jesus Christ your Son our Lord,
who is alive and reigns with you,
in the unity of the Holy Spirit,
one God, now and for ever.

Collect for the Nineteenth Sunday after Trinity,
Common Worship

Tuesday

Lord, be within me to strengthen me,
without me to preserve me,
over me to shelter me,
beneath me to support me,
before me to direct me,
behind me to bring back,
round about me to fortify.

Lancelot Andrewes (1555–1626)

Wednesday

Strengthen us, O God, to relieve the oppressed,
to hear the groans of poor prisoners,
to reform the abuses of all professions;
that many be made not poor to make a few rich:
for Christ's sake.

Oliver Cromwell (1599–1658)

Thursday

Thou hast given so much to me;
give one thing more, a grateful heart.
Not thankful when it pleases me,
as if thy blessings had spare days;
but such a heart whose very pulse
may be thy praise.

George Herbert (1593–1633)

Friday

Stay with me, Lord Jesus,
so that I shall begin to shine as you shine,
as light to others.
The light will be all from you.
It will be you who shine through me upon others.
Give light to them as well as to me;
light them with me, through me.
Help me to witness to you without preaching;
not by word but by example
and by the sympathetic influence of what I do;
by my visible resemblance to your saints
and the evident fullness of my love for you.

John Henry Newman (1801–1890)

Saturday

Give us grace, Almighty Father,
to address thee with all our hearts
as well as with our lips.
Thou art everywhere present:
from thee no secrets can be hidden.
Teach us to fix our thoughts on thee,
reverently and with love,
so that our prayers are not in vain,
but are acceptable to thee, now and always,
through Jesus Christ our Lord.

Jane Austen (1775–1817)

Fifth week of Lent – The power of God

Sunday

Most merciful God,
who by the death and resurrection
of your Son Jesus Christ
delivered and saved the world:
grant that by faith in him who suffered on the cross
we may triumph in the power of his victory;
through Jesus Christ your Son our Lord,
who is alive and reigns with you,
in the unity of the Holy Spirit,
one God, now and for ever.

Collect for the Fifth Sunday of Lent,
Common Worship

Monday

O God,
the strength of all those who put their trust in you,
mercifully accept our prayers
and, because through the weakness of our mortal nature
we can do no good thing without you,
grant us the help of your grace,
that in the keeping of your commandments
we may please you both in will and deed;
through Jesus Christ your Son our Lord,
who is alive and reigns with you,
in the unity of the Holy Spirit,
one God, now and for ever.

Collect for the First Sunday after Trinity,
Common Worship

Tuesday

Almighty God,
you see that we have no power of ourselves
to help ourselves:
keep us both outwardly in our bodies
and inwardly in our souls;
that we may be defended from all adversities
which may happen to the body,
and from all evil thoughts
which may assault and hurt the soul;
through Jesus Christ our Lord.

Post-Communion Collect for the Second Sunday of Lent,
Common Worship

Wednesday

Grant, O Lord, your protection;
and in your protection, strength;
and in your strength, understanding;
and in understanding, knowledge;
and in knowledge, the knowledge of justice;
and in the knowledge of justice, the love of it;
and in that love, the love of existence;
and in the love of all existence, the love of God,
God in all goodness.

Early Welsh

Thursday

O God,
you know us to be set
in the midst of so many dangers,
that by reason of the frailty of our nature
we cannot always stand upright:
grant us such strength and protection
as may support us in all dangers
and carry us through all temptations;
through Jesus Christ your Son our Lord,
who is alive and reigns with you,
in the unity of the Holy Spirit,
one God, now and for ever.

Collect for Fourth Sunday before Lent,
Common Worship

Friday

We beseech you, Master,
to be our helper and protector.
Save the afflicted among us;
have mercy on the lowly;
raise up the fallen;
appear to the needy;
heal the ungodly;
restore the wanderers of thy people;
feed the hungry;
ransom our prisoners;
raise the sick;
comfort the faint-hearted.

St Clement of Rome (First century)

Saturday

God of might and powerfulness,
here in love and gentleness,
protect me by your goodness
from each act of sinfulness,
from each word of hurtfulness,
from each thought of evilness.
By your presence and your holiness
surround me with your gracefulness.

David Adam

Palm Sunday

Lord Jesus,
as you were welcomed
when you entered into Jerusalem
with palms and shouts of praise,
we rejoice in your coming to us this day
and pray that you may enter into our lives
and the life of our community
as our Lord and King;
to you be all glory and honour,
who lives and reigns with the Father
and the Holy Spirit,
one God, now and for ever.

David Adam

Holy Week

Monday

Lord,
as I remember the cleansing of the Temple,
cleanse my heart and mind
from all evil desires and thoughts.
Cleanse from your Church all that is corrupt,
that it may be a true house of prayer,
and proclaim your glory in all the world;
for your glory and for your name's sake,
Jesus my Lord and my God.

David Adam

Tuesday

Lord,
as I remember today your meeting
with the disciples on the Mount of Olives,
fill my mind with the good news of the gospel
and make me aware of your power to save,
for you alone are my Lord and Saviour,
living and reigning with the Father
and the Holy Spirit,
one God, now and for ever.

David Adam

Wednesday

Lord,
who rested this day at Bethany
and prepared for what lay ahead,
make me mindful of your presence
in my home and in my life.
May I not be tempted to betray you,
and may I ever be mindful
of your friendship and love;
for your glory and for your name's sake,
Jesus my Lord and my God.

David Adam

Maundy Thursday

Lord Jesus,
as I remember your washing of the disciples' feet,
keep me humble and ready to serve.
As I remember the Last Supper,
make me aware of your coming in the sacrament
of the Eucharist.
As I remember your betrayal,
keep my heart and life loyal to you, Christ my Lord,
who lives and reigns with the Father
and the Holy Spirit,
one God, for ever and ever.

David Adam

Good Friday

O Saviour of the world,
who redeemed us by your cross and precious blood,
save us and help us, we humbly beseech you, O Lord.

From the Western Rite Liturgy

The cross of Christ
defend you from all evil,
strengthen your love for him,
keep you firm in the faith,
give you comfort in your sorrows,
and rescue you from death.

David Adam

Salvator Mundi

Jesus, Saviour of the world,
come to us in your mercy:
we look to you to save and help us.

By your cross and your life laid down,
you set your people free:
we look to you to save and help us.

When they were ready to perish,
you saved your disciples:
we look to you to come to our help.

In the greatness of your mercy,
loose us from our chains:
forgive the sins of all your people.

Make yourself known as our Saviour
and mighty deliverer:
save and help us that we may praise you.

Come now and dwell with us,
Lord, Jesus Christ:
hear our prayer and be with us always.

And when you come in your glory,
make us to be one with you
and to share the life of your kingdom.

Daily Prayer, Common Worship

Holy Saturday

Grant, Lord,
that we who are baptised into the death
of your Son our Saviour Jesus Christ
may continually put to death our evil desires
and be buried with him;
and that through the grave and gate of death
we may pass to our joyful resurrection;
through his merits,
who died and was buried and rose again for us,
your Son Jesus Christ our Lord.

Collect for Easter Eve, Common Worship

Early Easter morning

Rejoice, heavenly powers! Sing, choirs of angels!
Exult, all creation around God's throne!
Jesus Christ our King is risen!
Sound the trumpets of salvation!

Rejoice, O earth, in shining splendour,
radiant in the brightness of your King!
Christ has conquered! Glory fills you!
Darkness vanishes for ever!

On this holy night all evil is dispelled,
guilt is washed away, and peace restored.
So we are reconciled with God.
Alleluia!

From the Exsultet from the Easter Vigil

Easter Day

Today we rejoice in the salvation of the world.
Christ is risen; let us arise with him!
Christ enters new life; let us live in him!
Christ is come forth from the tomb;
let us shake off the fetters of evil!
The gates of hell are open,
the powers of evil are overcome!
In Christ a new creation is coming to birth,
Alleluia!
Let us make new.
Alleluia!

St Gregory of Nazianzus (c.330–389)

Yesterday I was crucified with Christ;
today I am glorified with him.
Yesterday I was dead with Christ;
today I am sharing in his resurrection.
Yesterday I was buried with him;
today I am waking with him from the sleep of death.

St Gregory of Nazianzus (c.330–389)

May the bright Light of Christ,
who is risen in glory,
scatter the darkness from our hearts and minds
and from this world.

David Adam

Easter Week

God of life,
who for our redemption gave your only begotten Son
to death on the cross,
and by his glorious resurrection
have delivered us from the power of our enemy:
grant us to die daily unto sin,
that we may evermore live with him
in the joy of his risen life;
through Jesus Christ our Lord.

Gregorian Sacramentary

I arise today with the power of God to guide me,
the might of God to uphold me,
the wisdom of God to teach me,
the eye of God to look over me,
the ear of God to hear me,
the word of God to give me speech,
the hand of God to protect me,
the path of God to lie before me,
the shield of God to shelter me,
the host of God to defend me against the snares
of the devil
and the temptations of the world,
against every one who meditates injury to me,
whether far or near.
I arise today.

Attributed to St Patrick (373–461)

Blessed be the God and Father of our Lord Jesus Christ!
By his great mercy he has given us
a new birth into a living hope
through the resurrection of Jesus Christ from the dead,
into an inheritance that is imperishable,
undefiled and unfading,
kept in heaven for us,
who are being protected by the power of God
through faith.
Blessed be God for ever.

Based on 1 Peter 1:3-5

Death has been swallowed up in victory.
Thanks be to God, who gives us the victory
through our Lord Jesus Christ.
We know that our labour is not in vain in the Lord.
Alleluia.

Based on 1 Corinthians 15:53, 57, 58

Goodness is stronger than evil;
love is stronger than hate;
light is stronger than darkness;
life is stronger than death;
victory is ours through him who loves us.

Desmond Tutu, An African Prayer Book (1995)

All shall be Amen and Alleluia.
We shall rest and we shall see,
we shall see and we shall know,
we shall know and we shall love,
we shall love and we shall praise.
Behold our end which is no end.

St Augustine of Hippo (354–430)

Almighty Father,
who in your great mercy gladdened the disciples
with the sight of the risen Lord:
give us such knowledge of his presence with us,
that we may be strengthened and sustained
by his risen life
and serve you continually in righteousness and truth;
through Jesus Christ your Son our Lord,
who is alive and reigns with you,
in the unity of the Holy Spirit,
one God, now and for ever.

Collect for the Third Sunday of Easter,
Common Worship